CD INCLUDED

HAL•LEONARD
BIG BAND PLAY-ALONG
VOLUME 2

PIANO

Popular Hits

ISBN-13: 978-1-4234-2232-7
ISBN-10: 1-4234-2232-5

HAL•LEONARD®
CORPORATION

7777 W. BLUEMOUND RD. P.O. BOX 13819 MILWAUKEE, WI 53213

Visit Hal Leonard Online at
www.halleonard.com

Hal • Leonard
BIG BAND PLAY-ALONG
VOLUME 2

CD INCLUDED

Popular Hits

AIN'T NO MOUNTAIN HIGH ENOUGH

Words and Music by
NICKOLAS ASHFORD and VALERIE SIMPSON
Arranged by ROGER HOLMES

PIANO

4

BRICK HOUSE

PIANO

Words and Music by LIONEL RICHIE, RONALD LaPREAD,
WALTER ORANGE, MILAN WILLIAMS,
THOMAS McCLARY and WILLIAM KING
Arranged by PAUL MURTHA

PIANO

PIANO

COPACABANA
(At The Copa)

Piano

Words by BRUCE SUSSMAN and JACK FELDMAN
Music by BARRY MANILOW
Arranged by JOHN BERRY

PIANO

PIANO

Recorded by SANTANA

EVIL WAYS

Words and Music by SONNY HENRY
Arranged by ROGER HOLMES

PIANO

I HEARD IT THROUGH THE GRAPEVINE

PIANO

Words and Music by
NORMAN J. WHITFIELD and BARRETT STRONG
Arranged by JOHN BERRY

Recorded by GEORGE BENSON

on broadway

PIANO

Words and Music by
**BARRY MANN, CYNTHIA WEIL,
MIKE STOLLER and JERRY LEIBER**
Arranged by JOHN HIGGINS

PIANO

Recorded by ARETHA FRANKLIN

RESPECT

Words and Music by
OTIS REDDING

Arranged by PAUL MURTHA

Piano

STREET LIFE

Words and Music by
WILL JENNINGS and JOE SAMPLE
Arranged by RICK STITZEL

Piano

PIANO

YESTERDAY

Words and Music by
JOHN LENNON and PAUL McCARTNEY
Arranged by JOHN BERRY

Piano

PIANO

PIANO

PIANO

Recorded by THE CHERRY POPPIN' DADDIES

ZOOT SUIT RIOT

PIANO

Words and Music by STEVE PERRY
Arranged by PAUL MURTHA